CRITICAL  TIMES

Peter Brookes

With a foreword by Daniel Finkelstein

Biteback Publishing

First published in Great Britain in 2019 by
Biteback Publishing Ltd
Westminster Tower
3 Albert Embankment
London SE1 7SP
Copyright © Peter Brookes 2019

Peter Brookes has asserted his right under the Copyright, Designs and
Patents Act 1988 to be identified as the author of this work.

ISBN 978-1-78590-520-9

10 9 8 7 6 5 4 3 2 1

A CIP catalogue record for this book is available from the British Library.

Set in Baskerville

Printed and bound in Great Britain by
CPI Group (UK) Ltd, Croydon CR0 4YY

MIX
Paper from
responsible sources
FSC
www.fsc.org   FSC® C020471

FOREWORD
By Daniel Finkelstein

One of the advantages of working for *The Times* – the oldest continuous daily newspaper in the world – is that as a writer and an editor you can go back and have a look at how your predecessors covered some of the great events in history – the Battle of Trafalgar, for instance, or the start of World War II.

Whenever I get out one of these old editions to study it, I am always struck by two things. The first is how much better the modern newspaper is. How much fuller, more direct, more accessible and more accurate it is. This is counter-intuitive because of folk memories of the paper's pre-eminence, but it is undeniable when you have two copies of the paper side by side.

The second is how dominant in the contemporary paper are the cartoons of Peter Brookes. They are the signature, really, of *The Times* in the modern age. Not just because of their visual impact, but because they express its spirit. Its wit, its political sophistication and its humanity. Everything we try to capture in words, Peter captures in his cartoons every day.

I have been Peter's colleague for almost twenty years, and for a period of that I was, as head of the comment desk, his editor. I say that, but most days that task involved staring in admiration at what he proposed to do and then affirming later that he had done it brilliantly. Editing is a very fancy word for that. But it did give me a little insight into how the cartoons in this book were produced and why they work.

Every weekday morning (arrangements are different on weekends), the senior staff of *The Times* meet to consider what might be contained in the next day's paper. Everyone is provided with a schedule that has been prepared by the various departments (home news, foreign, business, sport and so on). This contains a mixture of the big events we expect that day (a vote in the Commons, a court case to end) and exclusive news from our specialist correspondents.

Things might happen later that change the paper profoundly, but the morning meeting (or conference, as it is called) remarkably often describes the shape of the next day's *Times*.

Most of the contributing staff sit at the conference table, but one important participant sits in the corner, just past the editor's right shoulder. He says nothing but can sometimes be seen doodling with a pencil on his copy of the schedule. Peter's attendance is the most constant but unobtrusive feature of the *Times* conference.

It's important to describe this because central to the cartoons in this book is that they are a commentary on the day's news. It's a tribute to the skill of their execution and the profundity of the statements they make that they endure and make sense in this volume. But they all arise out of what is happening. As much as a photograph, they are a snapshot of that day's news. And as much as a comment column, they provide an insight into them that mere reporting can't. (I say mere reporting, but succinct, original and accurate reporting is very skilled work indeed.)

There are big differences between column writing and the artistry of the cartoon, but also one striking similarity. A successful column can't work without a big, central idea. The idea has to be powerful, convincing and the product of knowledge and (at least to a large group of readers, since you will never please everyone) an attractive and reasonably consistent world view.

Sometimes success lies in making people reflect that 'I never looked at it that way' and sometimes in the opposite: 'You've captured exactly what I think.' You can't be predictable, but you don't want to be so original that you are confusing.

The extraordinary skill of Peter Brookes allows him to achieve this success with remarkable consistency. He understands politics and world affairs as well as any of the commentators on the paper. He has a mind that allows him to summarise events in a single image, often bringing together two quite disparate events.

He brings to this his humanity. I don't always agree with Peter. Sometimes I think him Britain's wrongest man (although I often reflect later that it was me who was wrong). But his liberal outlook, his resolute opposition to cruelty, violence and hypocrisy, is compelling and attractive even when the reader disagrees.

And like the best of columnists he, of course, adds wit. Not just a clever interpretation but a funny one, too.

All this and he can draw. It is this that I think elevates Peter from being clearly pre-eminent among his contemporaries to being someone who can be classed with the real greats. With Gillray and Hogarth and Low (and Vicky, although I don't think Vicky is as good as these others or as Peter).

Actually, of course, it's not just drawing. Peter's use of colour is spectacular. He has told me that he was uncertain, when *The Times* became a colour paper, whether it would suit his style. But now his use of it is a joy, and one of the joys of this book.

Look at the cartoons of Donald Trump and Boris Johnson in this book, in which they are dominant characters. They are captured so well, the details and the sweep. The contrast between the American effort to save Europe and its current President's self-absorbed slogan seen side by side makes you laugh and wish to weep at the same time. As does the famous photograph of Boris Johnson with his lover, in which the lover is himself. Has anyone ever captured that facet of Boris so well?

I regarded Peter's ability to capture what people look like as so uncanny that I developed a joke in which, when he showed me his preliminary sketch, I would pretend that I couldn't recognise who it was. That was literally never the case. Peter did some cartoons that centred on one of my best friends. He observed and accentuated a feature of his face I hadn't even noticed, though I had known my friend by that point for more than a decade.

Do two things with this book. Enjoy it and keep it. Enjoy it because there is so much here to laugh at and to think about. Keep it because you are holding in your hands something our descendants will prize as a portrait of the age.

Daniel Finkelstein
London, 2019

Myanmar's ruler, Nobel Peace Prize laureate Aung San Suu Kyi, cancels her visit
to the UN amid attacks on Rohingya villages by the military.

Trump delivers his maiden address to the UN General Assembly.

Boris Johnson faces calls to be sacked after breaching the ministerial code. *Playboy* magazine founder Hugh Hefner dies.

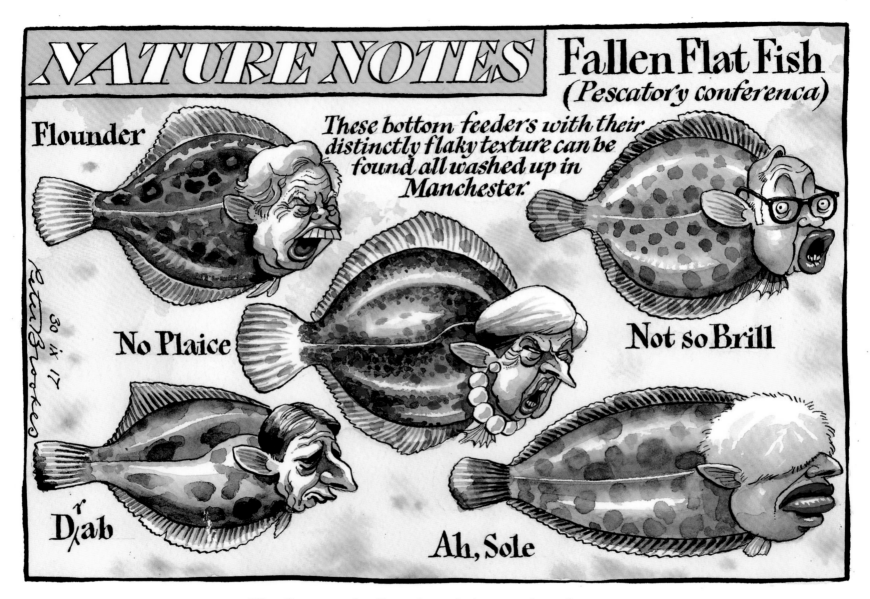

The Conservative Party host their annual conference.

Theresa May's keynote conference address, marred by her persistent cough, is overshadowed by a speech by Boris Johnson.

Xi Jinping becomes China's most powerful communist leader since Mao Zedong,
as his political philosophy is enshrined in the constitution.

May's Cabinet disintegrates as two ministers resign, a third is implicated in Westminster's sexual harassment scandal and a fourth faces renewed calls for his sacking.

Donald Trump lavishes praise on Xi Jinping during a state visit to Beijing.

END OF THE ROAD FOR MUGABE...

President Robert Mugabe is confined to his house as Zimbabwe's army mounts a military takeover.

EXPLORER FINDS TRIBE CUT OFF FROM REAL WORLD...

Jungle explorer Benedict Allen is 'rescued' from Papua New Guinea by the
Daily Mail, while the Tory Party seek out a plan for Brexit.

Theresa May issues a muted rebuke to Donald Trump after he retweets posts from the far-right Britain First party.

Donald Trump formally recognises Jerusalem as Israel's capital.

As HMS *Queen Elizabeth* is commissioned, the EU's chief negotiator tells
Theresa May she has just forty-eight hours to agree a potential deal.

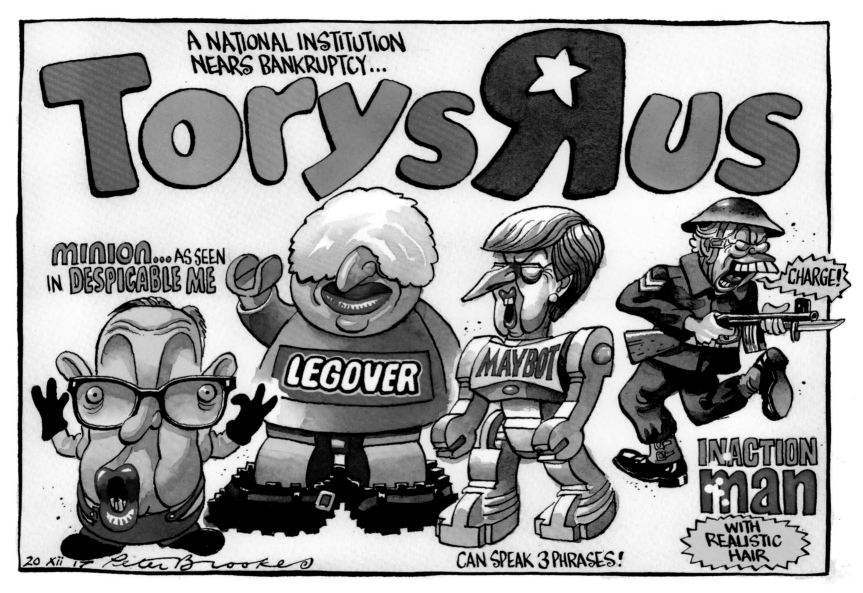

The Tory Party fear splits over a no-deal Brexit, while Toys 'R' Us faces collapse.

The government announces that UK passports issued after October 2019 will have blue covers. Damian Green resigns from the Cabinet after making misleading statements about pornography found on his House of Commons computer.

Michael Wolff releases *Fire and Fury*, his sensational exposé of the Trump White House.

Emmanuel Macron agrees to lend the Bayeux tapestry to Britain for the first time in its 950-year history.

May and Trump attend the World Economic Forum in Davos, while allegations emerge that waitresses at the men-only Presidents Club gala dinner were groped and harassed.

18

Trump asks the Pentagon to organise a large military parade in Washington, after being impressed by a Bastille Day parade in Paris the previous year.

RAMAPHOSA...

Cyril Ramaphosa becomes South Africa's new President and vows to fight corruption.

Following a Florida school shooting, Donald Trump bans lethal bump-fire stocks
but rejects all other gun controls and proposes arming teachers.

Russia refuses to support a UN ceasefire resolution in eastern Ghouta, describing reports of civilian casualties in Syria as 'mass psychosis'.

As Crown Prince Mohammed bin Salman visits London, Theresa May faces an outcry over the UK selling arms to Saudi Arabia while sending aid to Yemeni victims of Saudi bombing.

Trump arranges to meet North Korea's Kim Jung-un for a 'milestone' summit.

Sky football pundit Jamie Carragher is suspended for spitting at a young girl through a car window. Meanwhile, Vladimir Putin denies any involvement in the Skripal poisonings.

Mark Zuckerberg breaks his silence on the Cambridge Analytica
scandal after Facebook's value plunges by $58 billion.

Labour MPs accuse Jeremy Corbyn of failing to take action over antisemitism within the party.

Corbyn apologises for defending an antisemitic mural in east London. Christine Shawcroft resigns as head of the Labour Party's disputes panel.

Pope Francis appears to suggest to a journalist that Hell doesn't exist. Meanwhile, the countdown to Brexit continues.

Theresa May apologises to Caribbean leaders for the Windrush scandal, promising that no one will be deported.

Senior Labour MPs rally around Jeremy Corbyn during a Commons debate on antisemitism.

Commonwealth leaders agree to honour the Queen's 'sincere wish' for Prince Charles to succeed her as head of the Commonwealth.

President Macron enjoys the first official state visit of the Trump presidency.

Amber Rudd faces calls to resign over the Windrush scandal after falsely
claiming that immigration removal targets did not exist.

34

Theresa May reshuffles her Cabinet following Amber Rudd's resignation over the Windrush scandal.

Trump announces that the US will no longer abide by the Joint Comprehensive Plan of Action on Iran.

The royal family host Prince Harry and Meghan Markle's wedding at Windsor Castle.

Foreign Secretary Boris Johnson says he 'probably needs' a private
'Brexit plane' to help boost the UK's trade prospects.

Speaker John Bercow faces allegations of bullying by former staff. England footballer
Raheem Sterling defends his tattoo following tabloid criticism.

As his summit with Kim Jong-un draws near, Donald Trump holds a prison reform summit with reality TV star Kim Kardashian West, who requests clemency for a 63-year-old grandmother.

The World Cup kicks off in Russia, while Vladimir Putin continues to pursue
aggressive military policies in Syria, Ukraine and the Crimea.

Theresa May dismisses calls to legalise cannabis following an outcry when a child was hospitalised after his medicinal cannabis oil was seized at Heathrow Airport.

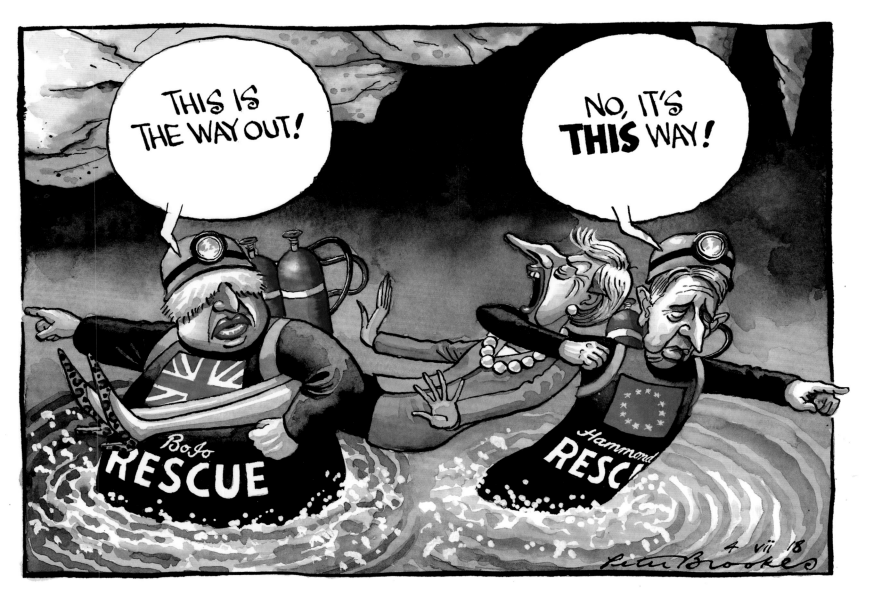

An international team struggle to rescue members of a junior football club trapped in a cave in Thailand. May's 'compromise' customs plan sparks Tory infighting.

43

May announces that the Cabinet has reached a 'collective' agreement
on the UK's relationship with the EU after Brexit.

Boris Johnson resigns as Foreign Secretary.

Trump attacks his European allies ahead of a NATO summit, claiming that
'frankly, Putin may be the easiest' part of his European itinerary.

At a joint summit with Vladimir Putin in Helsinki, Trump denies
that Russia interfered in the 2016 US presidential election.

Under fire from MPs, May insists that any Brexit deal must be 'workable' and
protect the UK economy as well as honouring the referendum result.

OPENING PARTNERSHIP...

Imran Khan claims victory in Pakistan's election amid accusations of vote rigging.

Theresa May visits Austrian Chancellor Sebastian Kurz in a bid to advance her proposals for a post-Brexit trade deal.

Trump returns the White House flag to half-mast after he faces criticism
for prematurely raising it following John McCain's death.

Two Russian nationals, thought to be military intelligence officers, are named as suspects in the Skripal poisonings. Labour's governing body argue over the definition of antisemitism.

Boris Johnson and Marina Wheeler announce they are divorcing, following rumours of Johnson having had another extramarital affair.

#WeTwo

The Senate Judiciary Committee approves Trump's nomination of Brett Kavanaugh to the Supreme Court, pending an FBI investigation into sexual assault claims against the judge.

Crown Prince Mohammed bin Salman denies Saudi involvement in the murder of journalist
Jamal Khashoggi, who disappeared from the Saudi consulate in Istanbul.

Banksy's *Girl With Balloon* self-destructs after being sold at auction for £1 million.
Theresa May considers delaying the UK's departure from the EU.

The world's oldest known intact shipwreck, dating back 2,400 years, is discovered at the bottom of the Black Sea.

Theresa May faces continued hostility to her Brexit plan after presenting the draft agreement to the Commons.

Theresa May survives a vote of no confidence in her leadership orchestrated by Jacob Rees-Mogg.

A pair of rogue drones shut down Gatwick Airport, sparking travel chaos.

Tory MP Anna Soubry is verbally abused by Brexit supporters with far-right links on College Green.

After the Commons votes to reopen negotiations on the Brexit deal, European Commission President Jean-Claude Juncker insists the EU will not renegotiate.

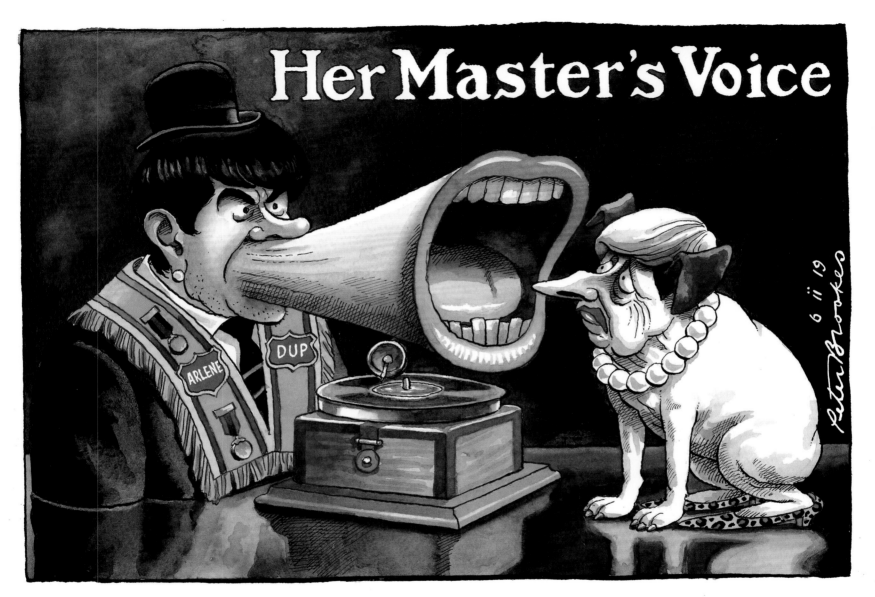

As May delivers a speech in Belfast, Arlene Foster insists that the Democratic Unionist Party won't tolerate a backstop to avoid a hard border in Northern Ireland.

European Council President Donald Tusk says there is a 'special place in hell' for Brexiteers with no plan.

Theresa May meets with EU leaders in a bid to negotiate changes to the withdrawal agreement.

Jeremy Corbyn writes to the Prime Minister setting out Labour's five demands for backing her Brexit deal, while facing criticism for opposing sanctions against Venezuela.

Shamima Begum, a pregnant British teenager who left the UK in 2015 to join
Islamic State, appeals to be allowed to 'come home and live quietly'.

Donald Trump declares a national emergency at the Mexican border
in order to access the funding needed to build a border wall.

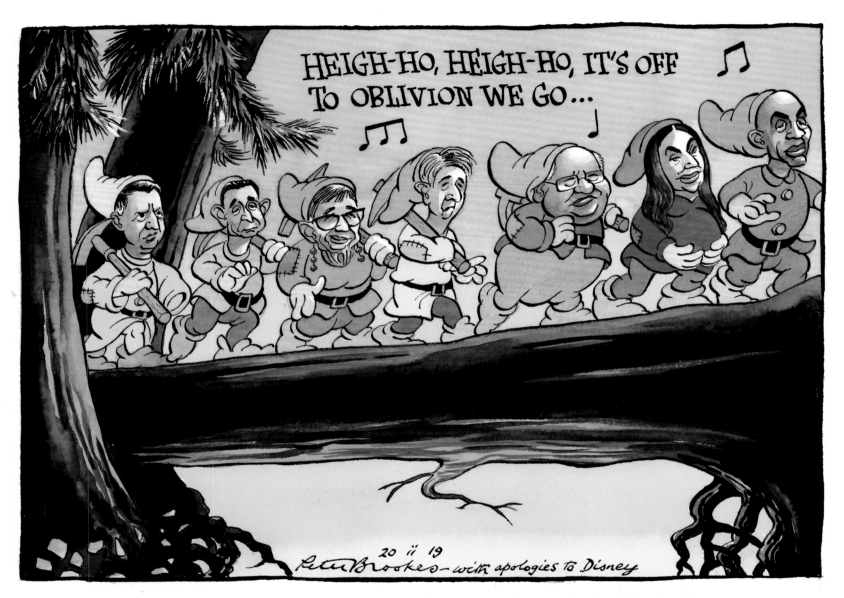

Seven Labour MPs resign from the party in protest at Jeremy Corbyn's leadership,
forming The Independent Group, later known as Change UK.

Donald Trump's second summit with Kim Jung-un is abruptly cut short.

Theresa May insists that there is no link between cuts to police numbers and a rise in knife crime.

The US ambassador to the UK urges Britain to accept American farming standards after Brexit, dismissing health fears over chlorinated chicken.

Theresa May asks to extend the Brexit deadline until 30 June.

EU leaders grant the Prime Minister an extension to 22 May if MPs back her deal, or 12 April if they don't.

MPs seek to seize control of the Brexit process, holding a series of indicative votes on alternatives to May's deal.

Footage emerges of soldiers using a Jeremy Corbyn poster for target practice. May meets with Corbyn to discuss possible compromises for a withdrawal agreement.

Theresa May requests a further Brexit extension until 30 June.

May meets European leaders to present her Brexit Plan B.

A new species of early human is discovered in the Philippines. Theresa May goes back
to Brussels for an emergency summit on extending the Brexit deadline.

As fire devastates Notre Dame Cathedral, questions are raised about the safety of the Houses of Parliament.

The Mueller Report is released, finding insufficient evidence to conclude
that Trump obstructed justice or conspired with Russia.

Emma Thompson flies from LA to London to join the Extinction
Rebellion protests calling for action on climate change.

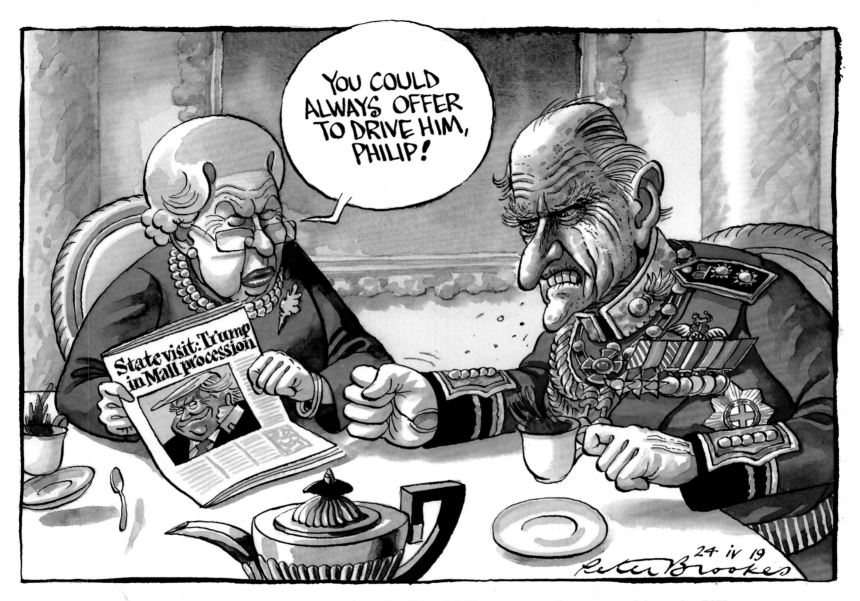

Buckingham Palace announces plans for Donald Trump to make a state visit to the UK.

Former Tory MP Ann Widdecombe defects to the Brexit Party to stand in the European elections.

the **Usual Suspects** PG

A number of Cabinet ministers publicly deny leaking information on the government's plans to allow Huawei to help build the UK's new 5G network.

Nigel Farage announces that the Brexit Party will stand in the next general election. Two dead crows are left strung up outside environmentalist Chris Packham's gate.

An Anglo-Saxon burial chamber described as Britain's version
of Tutankhamun's tomb is uncovered in Southend-on-Sea.

Leave-supporting Tory MPs object to the Prime Minister holding cross-party talks on Brexit.

Theresa May sets a date for laying out her timetable for departure, and says she still has 'full confidence' in Chris Grayling despite a series of gaffes including rail chaos following new train timetables.

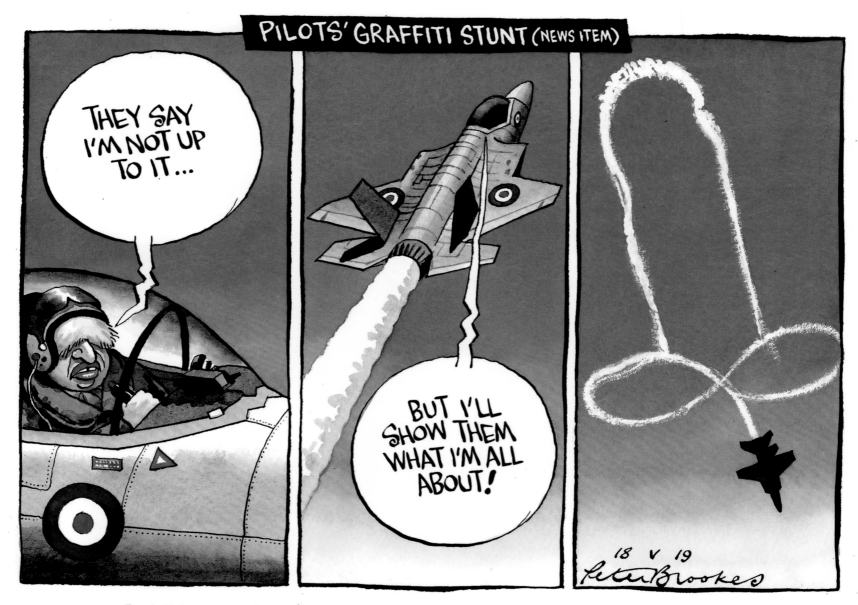

Boris Johnson confirms he will run for the Tory leadership on May's departure. The US Air Force claims a recent example of phallic skywriting was 'unintentional'.

The Brexit Party comes first in the European elections. Judith Kerr,
author of *The Tiger Who Came to Tea*, dies aged ninety-five.

Theresa May announces she will step down as Prime Minister on 7 June. A striking
photo reveals the extent of overcrowding on Mount Everest.

On his state visit to the UK, Donald Trump requests meetings with Michael Gove and Boris Johnson.

Trump joins the Queen and other world leaders in Portsmouth to honour the 75th anniversary of D-Day.

Boris Johnson launches his campaign to be the next Conservative Party leader.

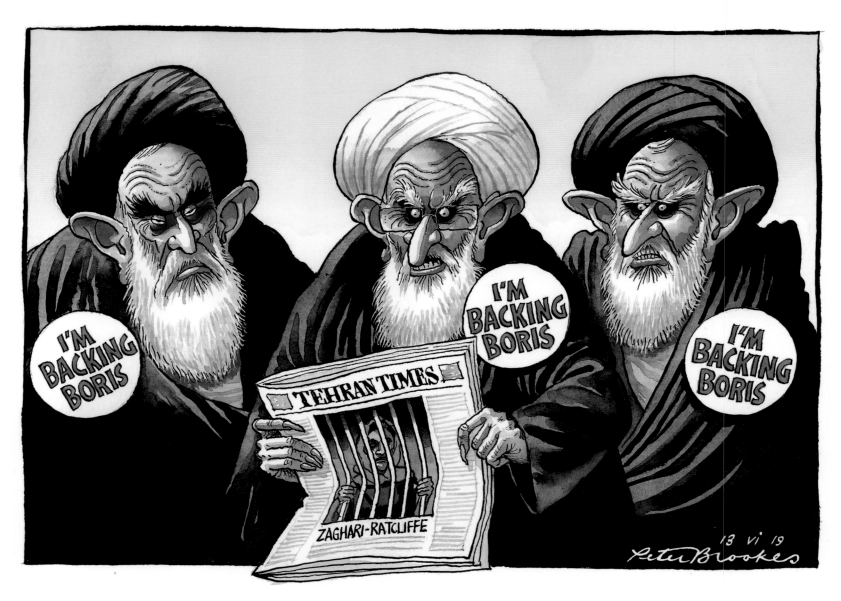

Johnson faces scrutiny of his record as Foreign Secretary as Nazanin Zaghari-Ratcliffe,
a British-Iranian charity worker, remains imprisoned in Iran after three years.

The first round of voting for the Tory leadership knocks out three contenders, leaving seven candidates in the race.

Boris Johnson is accused of hiding from media scrutiny after refusing to take part in Channel 4's leadership debate.

Jeremy Hunt makes it through to the final stage of the Conservative
leadership contest alongside hot favourite Boris Johnson.

Seemingly staged photos of Boris Johnson and partner Carrie Symonds are published
shortly after a row in which police were called to the couple's flat.

Amid widespread criticism, Chris Williamson is readmitted to the Labour Party
following his suspension over allegations of antisemitism.

4th JULY...

Donald Trump celebrates Independence Day with a military rally.

Boris Johnson claims to relax by crafting and painting model buses. Britain's US ambassador
Kim Darroch resigns following a row over leaked emails critical of Donald Trump.

JOHNSON'S SHUTDOWN THREAT BLOCKED...

MPs back an amendment stopping a new Prime Minister from suspending
Parliament to push through a no-deal Brexit.

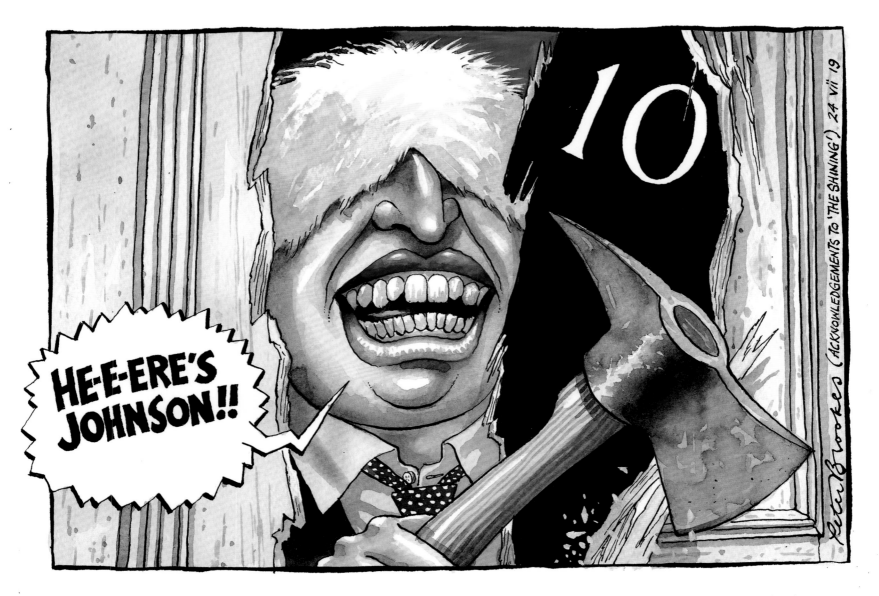

Boris Johnson becomes Prime Minister in waiting after winning the Conservative Party leadership election.

The Queen invites Boris Johnson to form a new government, amid speculation that his tenure may be short-lived.

Boris Johnson appoints a new Cabinet and assembles his leadership team.

US ambassador to the UK Woody Johnson says the new Prime Minister's relationship with Donald Trump will be 'sensational'.